9/01

Palo Alto City Library

The individual borrower is responsible for all library material borrowed on his or her card.

Charges as determined by the CITY OF PALO ALTO will be assessed for each overdue item.

Damaged or non-returned property will be billed to the individual borrower by the CITY OF PALO ALTO.

P.O. Box 10250, Palo Alto, CA 94303

SIERRA CLUB
WILDLIFE
LIBRARY
SHARKS

SIERRA CLUB WILDLIFE LIBRARY SHARKS

Eric S. Grace

Sierra Club Books for Children
San Francisco

The Sierra Club, founded in 1892 by John Muir, has devoted itself to the study and protection of the earth's scenic and ecological resources — mountains, wetlands, woodlands, wild shores and rivers, deserts and plains. The publishing program of the Sierra Club offers books to the public as a nonprofit educational service in the hope that they may enlarge the public's understanding of the Club's basic concerns. The point of view expressed in each book, however, does not necessarily represent that of the Club. The Sierra Club has some sixty chapters in the United States and in Canada. For information about how you may participate in its programs to preserve wilderness and the quality of life, please address inquiries to Sierra Club, 85 Second Street, San Francisco, CA 94105-3441.

First Edition

Photo Credits: © Brandon Cole: 1, 12, 24, 27, 29; © Bob Cranston: 8, 9, 15, 19, 23, 30, 35, 42; © Kip Evans: 3; © Tom Haight: 13, 20; © Eda Rogers: 10; © Josh Singer: 5, 16, 18, 33; © Marty Snyderman: 7, 36, 39, 45.

Library of Congress Cataloging-in-Publication data is available from Sierra Club Books for Children, 85 Second Street, San Francisco, CA 94105-3441.

First published in Canada by Key Porter Books Limited.

Printed and bound in Italy

10 9 8 7 6 5 4 3 2 1

Contents

The Most Fearsome Fish in the Ocean

The great white shark is suspended motionless in the gloomy water. Its lower jaw hangs slightly open under a bullet-shaped snout, showing rows of daggerlike teeth. Its powerful body is twice the length of the diver who faces it, eye to eye, with only a wall of clear plastic between them.

This remarkable scene was filmed by a team of shark researchers led by the well-known ocean explorer Jean-Michel Cousteau. For two-and-a-half years, the group of divers, scientists, and filmmakers gathered information about great white sharks off the southern coast of Australia, spending much of their time observing the giant fish underwater from a transparent plastic cylinder.

Their dramatic encounters with one of the world's most frightening predators made a lasting impression on the team members. After swimming with sharks at close quarters, they developed a new understanding and respect for them. "I can never again think of these sharks as being the crazed killers I once thought," said one diver who had come to know the animals at home in their own environment.

That doesn't mean great white sharks aren't dangerous. They are among the few large animals left on Earth that sometimes attack and kill people, and it's hard not to feel a shiver of dread at the sight of their long, sinister silhouettes.

Fortunately, researchers such as Cousteau and his team are helping to dispel our deep-seated fear of sharks, shedding light on these fascinating and seldom-seen animals. Thanks to their work, we now have a chance to understand sharks' behavior – to discover how they hunt, how far they travel, where they breed, and other details of their previously mysterious lives.

The great white shark is the largest carnivorous fish in the sea. It is greatly feared – and greatly misunderstood.

Although it is the largest of sharks, the whale shark feeds mostly on floating plankton.

The infamous great white shark is only one of about 350 species of sharks found in oceans around the world. (A few shark species live in freshwater rivers and lakes.) Not all of these sharks are fierce predators. The largest, the whale shark, is a harmless giant, measuring up to forty feet from snout to tail and feeding on plankton – candy-size floating organisms such as fish eggs, shrimp, larvae, and tiny fish. The smallest sharks can be held in the palm of a hand and feed on marine mollusks and worms.

Sharks are fish, but a particular class of fish, different from all others but their closest relatives – the skates, rays, and sawfish. Unlike the majority of fish, sharks and their relatives don't have hard, bony skeletons. Their skeletons are made of a softer, more flexible material called cartilage. Sharks get their scientific name from this fact and are placed in a class called Chondrichthyes (con-DRIC-thees), meaning "cartilaginous fish."

A second big difference between sharks and other fish is one you can see for yourself. All fish have gills, through which they breathe. A shark's gills open to the outside by vertical gill slits, located on each side of its body, just behind the head. In bony fish, the gills are covered by gill flaps, which the fish opens and closes to pump water across its gills. Sharks do not have these gill flaps.

All sharks, such as this six-gill shark, have from five to seven pairs of gill slits, which allow them to breathe.

Ancient teeth and scales found scattered on beaches or fossilized in prehistoric seabeds tell us what the ancestors of today's sharks were like. Those hard parts of their bodies are mostly all that remains of the long-ago predators, although a few fossils of whole sharks have been found in soft shale rock. The well-preserved relics dug from the ground are of creatures that died 350 million years ago. After death, their bodies sank quickly into the thick mud and sediment of the ocean floor, where they were protected from scavengers and decay and saved for immortality.

Because of their long history, sharks are sometimes called "primitive" fish, or "living fossils." This is not very accurate. Sharks and bony fish have been evolving along separate paths for more than 400 million years, and sharks as a group are not older than other fish. Sharks, however, have not developed so great a diversity as the bony fish. Some of today's sharks are similar in general appearance to the very first sharks, although they are more efficient swimmers and hunters.

Many of the earliest shark species had already become extinct as the Age of Dinosaurs was beginning, about 230 million years ago. This was a period when the oceans were undergoing great changes. Some of the most common types of sharks at that time specialized in feeding on hard-shelled animals that flourished in shallow seas. As the Earth's land mass split up and the continents began moving farther apart, large areas of

The slim leopard shark grows to five feet and feeds on fish and crustaceans.

shallow water were replaced by deeper oceans. As a result, many of the hard-shelled animals disappeared, and so did the sharks that depended on them.

Other types of sharks, with longer, streamlined bodies and rows of sharp, cutting teeth, began swimming the open oceans. The first modern sharks, including six-gill and horn sharks, appeared about 200 million years ago. By 100 million years ago, long before the last living dinosaurs vanished from the Earth, all the groups of sharks living today had evolved.

Based on their similarities and differences, scientists divide modern sharks into eight main groups, or orders (see page 11). More than three-quarters of all sharks are in just two of these orders: the Carcharhiniformes (large, open-ocean sharks) and Squaliformes (smaller, deeper-living sharks). The details of this classification change as scientists learn more about different species.

TYPES OF SHARKS

Hexanchiformes
This group includes six-gill and seven-gill sharks, the oldest group of sharks. They are generally slow-moving and live at great depths, and little is known about them. This group also includes the primitive frilled shark, a deep-sea species that feeds on squid.

Squaliformes
There are more than eighty species in this group, including bramble sharks, leopard sharks, and dogfish. They are smaller sharks, with two dorsal fins. Many of them live in cooler seas, and some species commonly travel together near the sea floor in large groups called schools.

Pristiophoriformes
Sawsharks are bottom-feeders that measure about four feet in length. Found mainly in southern oceans, they have long, flattened, beaklike snouts with toothed edges, like a saw.

Orectilobiformes
Nurse sharks (also called carpet sharks) are mostly sluggish animals, often found resting on the sea floor. They eat small fish, shrimp, crabs, and squid. This group includes zebra sharks and Australian wobbegongs. Other families in this group are the giant whale sharks and basking sharks.

Squatiniformes
Angel sharks (also called monkfish) look more like skates than sharks. They have flattened bodies, but their gill slits are located at the sides of their heads, not underneath as in skates and rays. Some species grow to eight feet in length.

Heterodontiformes
Horn sharks have high heads and two different shapes of teeth in their jaws. The front teeth are pointed for biting, and the side teeth are flattened and ridged for crushing shellfish. This type of shark was common more than 200 million years ago, and there are about ten species living today.

Carcharhiniformes
This is the largest group of sharks, with nearly 200 species. Most are big, powerful swimmers and hunters found far from shore in tropical waters, including gray sharks, blue sharks, reef sharks, tiger sharks, requiem sharks, and hammerheads. A few species live in freshwater lakes and rivers.

Lamniformes
The fastest and fiercest of sharks, these are known as mackerel sharks because they look like mackerel with their spindle shape, large eyes, and crescent-shaped tailfins. This group includes mako sharks, porbeagles, and great white sharks.

A sluggish nurse shark is accompanied by a group of pilot fish, which feed on skin parasites and leftover scraps of food.

A NEW SPECIES OF SHARK

A new deep-sea species was first discovered in 1976 near the Hawaiian island of Oahu. The odd-looking shark was more than fourteen feet long and weighed three-quarters of a ton. It had a large head with huge, gaping jaws that it used to scoop up shrimp and other small organisms. Called "megamouth" by the newspapers, the shark was so unlike others that scientists classified it in a family of its own. Since this discovery, four more of these rare sharks have been caught at sea or found washed ashore.

Some sharks are swift, active hunters in the open ocean; others are slow, sluggish creatures that spend much of their time resting near the ocean floor. Some sharks lay eggs, and some give birth to fully developed young. Only a few species of sharks have ever been studied in any detail, however, and little is known about the lives of most.

With the growing popularity of ocean diving and exploration, we are finding out more about different sharks all the time. And with better understanding comes a new appreciation. The old image of sharks as horror-movie monsters is slowly being replaced by admiration for these superbly adapted animals, shaped for survival in their underwater world.

13

The Body of a Shark

Designed like underwater flying machines, sharks are built to cruise effortlessly through the seas. Although capable of bursts of speed up to thirty miles per hour, sharks usually swim at a more leisurely pace over long distances. Stouter, blunter-headed sharks tend to be less active bottom feeders, while the jets of the shark world are tapered, long-bodied mackerel sharks, which hunt in the open seas for fast-swimming fish such as tuna and marlin.

Mackerel sharks are able to move and react swiftly thanks to a unique blood flow that keeps their swimming muscles several degrees warmer than the surrounding water – more like warm-blooded mammals than cold-blooded fish. A rich network of tiny arteries and veins supplies their deep-lying muscles and helps conserve body heat.

Lacking rigid, bony skeletons, sharks' bodies are tough and muscular. More than half a shark's weight is muscle, giving it great power and endurance – which it needs. A shark is heavier than sea water and must swim constantly to avoid slowly sinking to the ocean floor.

Helping to increase a shark's buoyancy is its huge, oil-rich liver. A shark's liver runs the length of its abdominal cavity and can make up as much as 30 percent of the animal's weight out of water. Since liver oil is five to six times more buoyant than sea water, this amount of oil in its body helps buoy the shark so that it can swim with less effort.

Like other fish, sharks breathe through their gills, absorbing oxygen from the water and releasing carbon dioxide as waste. Because they do not have gill flaps, sharks must keep water flowing over their gills by swimming. You may have heard people say that if a shark stops swimming it will drown. Sharks that become tangled in fishing nets do indeed drown very

The mako shark is a member of the mackerel shark group and is among the fastest swimmers of all sharks.

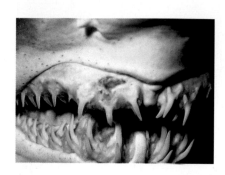

Sharks' teeth, like those of this sand tiger shark, evolved from scales.

quickly. But some bottom-dwelling sharks are often seen resting on the seabed. The answer may be that they are resting in a slow-flowing current or in oxygen-rich water, and when a shark is resting its breathing rate is very low.

A shark's skin is as rough as sandpaper, due to a covering of pointed scales that look and feel like tiny teeth. In fact, there's a close connection between a shark's scales and its teeth. Early in shark evolution, the scales lining the inner edges of the jaws helped sharks catch and hold their slippery prey. Over time, these scales became long and curved, eventually evolving into teeth.

Shark scales (called placoid scales) are similar in structure to human teeth, with an outer layer of hard, enamel-like substance, an inner layer of dentine, and a pulp cavity at the base with nerves and blood vessels. Scales are similar in size over most of the shark's body but can vary in shape. For example, they may be rounded on the snout and diamond-shaped along the front of the fins. The scales on fast-swimming sharks are spread apart to let the water flow easily past them, reducing the drag that would slow the shark down.

An expert can tell which type of shark a tooth comes from by the tooth's size and shape, which are suited to the feeding habits of the species. Most sharks have the curved, sharp, cutting teeth of predators, but those that feed on mollusks have low, rounded teeth for crushing shells. The huge jaws of plankton-feeding sharks have hundreds, or even thousands, of tiny, rasplike teeth no bigger than one-twelfth of an inch in length.

A shark's jaws may hold six or more rows of teeth. Only the outer one or two rows are functional, however. The other rows behind them are replacement teeth, which move to the outer edges of the jaws as the older teeth are lost through wear or accident. A shark loses about one tooth a week on average.

THE SHARK'S SPIRAL VALVE

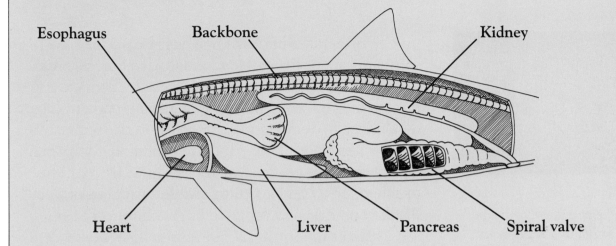

Esophagus   Backbone   Kidney

Heart   Liver   Pancreas   Spiral valve

The spiral valve inside a shark's intestine is shown here in a cutaway section. After food passes through the shark's esophagus and stomach, it is forced to follow the spiral path of the valve. By doing this, the food makes contact with a larger surface of intestine than it could by moving through a straight, smooth tube of the same length. Digestive enzymes from the pancreas and other glands help digest the food in this part of the digestive system. The digested food is absorbed into the bloodstream through the lining of the intestine.

Any unfortunate prey that enters a shark's jaws continues its journey to the stomach, where strong muscles and digestive juices break it into small pieces. Next, the food moves into an intestine with a unique design.

The intestine is where digested food is absorbed into the bloodstream. Many animals have very long, coiled intestines, giving them a big surface area through which nutrients can be absorbed for use by the body. The shark's intestine, however, is short and S-shaped. Inside, it contains a spiral valve along its length – like a screw tightly enclosed in a tube. Food must go around and around the path of the valve, rather like moving down a spiral ramp. This design gives the shark's intestine a much larger surface area on the inside than it would have if there were no valve.

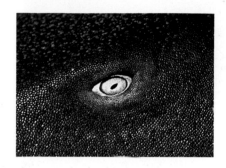

The pupil of a shark's eye may be round or slit, and alters in size according to the light level.

Do sharks drink? Strange as it may seem, most fish in the ocean face a problem of dehydration. Because sea water is saltier than the fluids inside a typical fish, water tends to be drawn out of the fish's body to create a balance. To compensate, bony fish in the sea restore their water by drinking a lot and producing only small amounts of urine. (Freshwater fish have the opposite problem. To avoid becoming swollen with water, they drink very little and produce large amounts of urine.)

Sharks differ from other marine fish, however, by having body fluids that are about as salty as sea water. It isn't sea salt in their blood but urea – a salt-like waste product that is normally concentrated in an animal's kidneys and is excreted from its body in urine. Rather than getting rid of urea, a shark's kidneys help retain a high level of it in the body. With blood about as salty as sea water, sharks are not at risk of dehydration and don't drink as much as other marine fish.

Sharks are commonly thought to lack intelligence, but studies show their brains and abilities are more complex than was once believed. Some species have a ratio of brain weight to body weight similar to that of birds and some mammals. Smaller species in captivity have been taught to remember different shapes and sounds. And active, hunting sharks need especially large brains to sense and pursue their prey in the open world of the ocean, where there are few landmarks and little or no light.

Sunlight penetrates the ocean to a depth of only about 400 feet. Below that, the ocean is pitch black. Like many animals that are active at night, some sharks have a mirrorlike layer at the back of their eyeballs that helps them see better in dim conditions. This layer reflects all the light that enters the eye back onto the retina, increasing the brightness of the image.

Sharks have either round or slit pupils that alter in size according to the light level. A shark's eyes are

particularly keen at picking out light colors, such as the pale flash of a fish belly. Some species have a protective membrane, like an eyelid, that covers each eye when they are about to bite into their prey.

To make up for their limited use of sight underwater, sharks have a very acute sense of smell. A large part of the shark's brain governs this sense, and many nerves connect the brain directly with a series of petal-like flaps located in the shark's nostrils. Sensitive cells on these flaps can detect even very small quantities of substances dissolved in the water flowing through a shark's nostrils, giving the shark the nickname of a "swimming nose."

Sharks have ears but no eardrums. The main structure of the inner ear is a set of three semicircular tubes used for the sense of balance. This inner-ear

Hunting sharks, such as this blue shark, use their acute sense of smell to detect prey over long distances.

19

Every shark, including this whitetip reef shark, has lateral lines running down its body that allow it to feel pressure waves in the water around it.

mechanism keeps the shark aware of its speed, its turns, and its movements up and down – vital knowledge in three-dimensional underwater space.

Like other underwater animals, sharks have a sense that can be called "hearing by touch" or "distant touch." They detect waves of pressure moving through the water just as our ears detect waves of pressure moving through the air. You can get an idea of how the shark's pressure sensors work the next time you're in a bathtub. Simply push one hand back and forth under the bathwater at one side of the tub and feel the water motion with the palm of your other hand at the other side.

Pressure waves (for example, those made by moving schools of fish or a splashing human swimmer) travel faster and farther through water than through air, allowing sharks to quickly sense movement or underwater sound from great distances away. Although a shark can feel pressure changes over most of its body, pressure sensors are concentrated along horizontal canals, called lateral lines, that run down both sides of its body from snout to tail. Nerve cells lining the canals have fine hairs that move with the water flow, signaling to the shark what's going on all around it. The size and speed of the pressure waves indicate such things as the distance to the object producing them and how big it is.

Another remarkable sense that sharks have is the ability to detect weak electric currents. They do this by means of tiny sensory pits scattered around their snouts. All living animals produce small electric fields, and the amount of current they generate increases if the animal is very active or injured. Researchers have found that sharks can use their electric sensors to locate a fish up to three feet away, even when the fish is hidden from sight under sand on the sea floor.

In one experiment, scientists suspended current-producing electrodes from a boat and pumped an odor of fish from a small container nearby. Sharks were drawn to the boat by the tempting smell, but after closing in, they tended to snap more often at the electrodes than at the source of the odor.

With their combined array of senses, it's not surprising that sharks appear very quickly on the scene whenever a fish is injured or struggling in the water. But there are still many mysteries about shark senses that researchers are trying to solve. For example, how do some species navigate over long distances during their annual migrations? Scientists have found that lemon sharks are able to return to the same place after being captured and moved to a distant location. They do this even if their eyes are covered, or their nostrils are blocked, or if they are moved in a box that masks the Earth's magnetic field! Exactly how, nobody yet knows.

The Hunters

Cruising slowly through shallow waters less than a mile from shore, the tiger shark feels an irregular pulse of pressure waves against its side. Turning sharply toward the source of the sensation, it gives a thrust of its powerful tail and speeds in a line just below the sun-dappled waves, its bladelike dorsal fin cutting now and then through the ocean surface.

The stream of salt water coursing through the shark's nostrils brings the odor of fish blood just a minute or so before it sees the shadowy shapes of other sharks circling ahead of it. The predators, large and small, are moving in from all sides now, focused on an injured tuna, the size of a man's leg, that has just pulled free from a fishing hook.

Slowly sinking into dimmer waters beneath the others, the tiger shark positions itself and then suddenly rises almost vertically to attack. First pushing the tuna forward with a sharp blow from its snout, the shark opens its jaws and bites deeply into the flesh. Giving a twist and turn to one side, it tears off a large chunk of fish and veers away. As if given a signal, other sharks dash to the now lifeless prey, snapping at the fish and one another with savage teeth.

The smell of fish blood and the sounds of thrashing excite the predators into a frenzy of activity. They whirl and pivot in tight circles, swinging their heads from side to side and biting anything in their path. Two sharks clash their jaws together and shake each other briefly before scooting apart, leaving strips of torn skin and broken teeth behind them.

The rest of the tuna has now disappeared down the gullets of two or three of the larger sharks. With the prey devoured, the smaller predators retreat, fearful for their own safety. The others make a few rapid crisscross passes where the tuna once was, keeping a careful

Though sharks sometimes feed together in large groups, as shown by these Caribbean reef sharks, for the most part they are solitary hunters.

Large open-ocean sharks, such as this tiger shark, prey on a wide variety of species.

distance from one another as they navigate like aircraft around a busy airport. One by one they turn away to resume their slower, solitary paths through the ocean.

Tales of feeding frenzies such as this are common enough in the folklore of sharks. They describe the pattern of feeding behavior that people are most likely to see when they throw dead fish or other bait over the sides of boats, attracting large numbers of sharks to investigate. These intense, shark-eat-shark gatherings add to sharks' notorious reputation for ferocity, but they are not the usual way sharks go about their daily search for food.

From time to time, when food is abundant in one particular area, sharks can be seen feeding together in large groups, sometimes made up of several different species. Some smaller sharks, such as dogfish, have also been known to hunt together in packs when attacking larger prey. For the most part, however, sharks search for food on their own.

The prey of large, open-ocean sharks includes bony fish, smaller sharks, turtles, squid, dolphins, crustaceans, seabirds, seals, and sea lions. Sharks generally eat whatever they can catch, although some species specialize in particular types of prey. Hammerhead sharks, for example, seem especially fond of stingrays.

A diver with the Cousteau research team was lucky enough to see a hammerhead catch and kill a stingray. The shark first used its head like a hammer to pound the stingray against the seabed and then took its time feasting on the large fish. Blacktip and sharpnose sharks attracted to the scene scavenged bits of the ray's carcass. Most sharks are opportunists and will readily take dead animals and leftovers from others' meals.

The hunting strategy of the dreaded great white shark, and perhaps other large predatory sharks, is to surprise its prey and disable it with the first massive bite before returning to finish it off. These sharks are

The strangely shaped head of the hammerhead shark may be used to stun prey on the sea floor.

SHARK TAILS

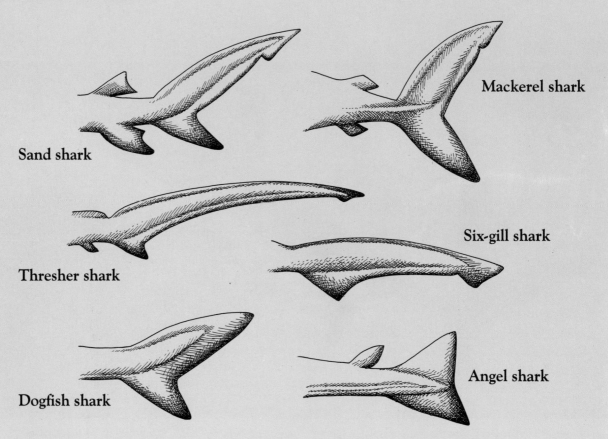

Sand shark

Mackerel shark

Thresher shark

Six-gill shark

Dogfish shark

Angel shark

Shark tails come in a range of shapes and sizes, related partly to the animal's speed and agility. In most sharks, the upper lobe of the tailfin is larger than the lower. The larger upper lobe would tend to pitch the front of the shark's body downward as it swims, but horizontal pectoral fins at the front of the body help keep the shark level. Many sharks have a notch in the upper lobe, but the function of this, if any, is not clear.

The most symmetrical tails, with both lobes of similar size, are found among fast swimmers such as mackerel sharks. The lower lobe acts as a keel that lets the fish make quick turns. Mackerel sharks tend to hold their streamlined bodies stiffly and let their powerful tails do all the work of swimming, using short, strong thrusts. Slower swimmers are more flexible, and their bodies undulate as they move.

The amazingly long upper lobe of the thresher shark's tail is about as long as the rest of the shark's body. The thresher shark splashes the water with its tail while swimming around a group of fish. It is thought that this may be a way of driving the fish into a compact mass to make them easier to prey on. The threshing tail may also make shock waves that help stun small fish.

colored dark on the back, shading to a light color on the belly. This pattern makes them difficult to see both from above (against the sea depths) and from below (against the sea surface and sky). With an incredible speed of attack, a great white shark can appear out of nowhere and shear off a large chunk of flesh in its massive jaws, all within less than two seconds. It's no wonder swimmers and surfers fear them.

Not all sharks are fierce, sharp-toothed hunters, however. Port Jackson sharks, for example, feed on shellfish, grinding them up with their flattened teeth. They are members of one of the older groups of sharks, usually found in shallow, tropical waters. They also feed on fish and sea urchins.

Perhaps the least shark-like of sharks are the filter-feeders – whale sharks, basking sharks, and megamouth sharks. The largest sharks in the world, they are docile and harmless creatures whose greatest threat to people might be colliding with a small boat. They feed on floating plankton, which they strain out of the water on comblike gill rakers in their gullets.

Port Jackson sharks have specialized teeth used for grinding and crushing shellfish.

27

Basking sharks, which can be up to twenty-three feet long, get their name from their habit of lying at the surface of the sea with their backs exposed, as if sunbathing. A feeding basking shark swims slowly with its enormous jaws wide open, letting water flow into its mouth, across its gill rakers, and out through its gill slits. When the gill rakers are clogged with trapped plankton, the shark swallows, pushing the food down its throat. Cruising like this, a basking shark can filter hundreds of thousands of gallons of sea water every hour, giving it enough small fish and shrimp to fuel its great bulk.

In fact, sharks eat far less than most people imagine. Being cold-blooded animals, they don't need food energy to keep their bodies warm. And with their efficient design, they use relatively little energy for swimming. A shark eats much less than a dolphin or sea lion of similar size, and a great white shark may be able to go without food for a month or two. Captive sharks are kept healthy on a diet of no more than 10 percent of their body weight per week, which is probably similar to their food intake in the wild.

Do sharks' predatory habits pose a major risk to human swimmers? Sharks attack some fifty to seventy-five people each year around the world, but the vast majority of victims live to tell the tale. According to records kept in the International Shark Attack File, not more than a dozen people are killed by sharks in a given year. That's many fewer than the number killed by elephants, bees, crocodiles, or lightning. To put it in perspective, as many people are killed by dogs in the United States in one year as have been killed by great white sharks in 200 years.

Despite these statistics, "Shark Attack!" is still a headline that sells newspapers and sends shivers down people's spines. Of the approximately 350 shark species, most are too small or inoffensive to harm people. Only

Although many sharks, including this oceanic whitetip, are deadly and well-equipped hunters, fewer than a dozen people are killed by sharks in any given year.

These Caribbean reef sharks are displaying the classic attack warning posture, with their backs arched and their fins pointed down.

thirty-two species are known to have attacked humans, the four most dangerous being the great white, bull, tiger, and oceanic whitetip. These are all large animals that normally eat prey similar in size to humans, and the first three hunt in shallow coastal waters, where swimmers are found.

From studies of shark behavior carried out in recent years, it seems likely that most attacks by sharks on people are cases of mistaken identity. A surfer lying on a surfboard with arms and legs over the side is about the same size and shape as a sea lion and might easily be confused with one from below the surface.

Scuba divers who have been attacked by sharks often report that the shark swam in a particular posture just before striking. It is a posture sharks use to warn away large fish and other sharks from their territories. In these cases, the attacking shark may be more intent on driving away an intruder than grabbing a human meal.

Although shark attacks can have very grisly results, surprisingly few are fatal, and it is extremely rare for a shark to completely devour someone. Sharks tend to lunge, bite, and swim off, rather than holding victims in their jaws. This leaves people with terrible gashes or missing limbs, but alive and able to survive if they can quickly get to a hospital before losing too much blood. The parts of the world where most shark attacks occur are along the coasts of California, Florida, Australia, and South Africa.

Are there any good shark repellents? Some experiments suggest sharks are attracted to light colors – especially yellow, white, and silver – so many divers recommend using dull-colored clothing, fins, and tanks to avoid shark attacks. Quiet movements are also less likely to attract a shark's attention than thrashing actions.

A type of sole that lives in the Red Sea and Indian Ocean seems naturally immune to shark attack. Named the Moses sole, it has poison glands in its skin that can kill other fish, and it is avoided by sharks. If scientists can analyze and make a synthetic form of the poisonous chemical, it could become an effective protection for divers and swimmers.

Reproducing
Their Kind

Here's how most marine fish reproduce. During the breeding season, a typical mother fish sheds many thousands of eggs into the sea, where they are fertilized by a shower of sperm from male fish and then left to drift away to their fates. The vast majority of those fertilized eggs, and the young fish that hatch from them, will be eaten by larger fish and other animals. Only one or two offspring from each set of parents will survive all hazards and grow over the months and years into adults, to eventually breed in their turn.

It may seem a wasteful way to continue the species, but it works. Two surviving offspring from each set of parents are all that's needed to keep the fish population at a steady level. And all those surplus eggs and small fish produced each year aren't really wasted. They play a vital part in the ocean's food chains. Little fish make meals for larger fish, which fall prey to still larger fish – including sharks.

At the top of many ocean food chains, sharks are much less numerous than their prey. They run little risk of being eaten once fully grown, and they don't need to produce such huge numbers of young in order to survive. In contrast to other fish, they have a very different strategy of reproduction.

Most sharks probably have breeding areas, where adult males and females gather to mate at a particular time of year. Outside their breeding season, they may swim over vast distances without meeting others of their kind for days or weeks.

Sharks must pair up to breed because, unlike other fish, the eggs are fertilized inside the female's body. Male sharks have structures called claspers for this purpose – a pair of long, cylindrical organs projecting from the male's pelvic fins. During mating,

This pregnant whitetip reef shark rests near the bottom of the ocean floor.

the male inserts one of these claspers into the female's genital opening to carry his sperm to her eggs.

The courtship and mating behavior of most shark species has never been seen, and the little we know about it comes mainly from observations of sharks in captivity. Full-grown male sharks of many species are about three-quarters the size of females. They grip the females with their mouths during mating, and many adult female sharks have scars from teeth marks on their backs as a result. In smaller, more flexible species, such as cat sharks and dogfish, males coil themselves around their partners to mate.

After mating, some shark species lay eggs; others keep the fertilized eggs in their bodies and later produce live young. Egg-laying sharks, such as horn sharks, swell sharks, and dogfish, seek out suitable, safe areas to deposit their few dozen eggs. They usually look for shallow, warm waters near the coast, where there is food for the newborn young. Most adult sharks stop feeding during the breeding season, perhaps so there is no risk they might eat their own offspring.

Shark eggs are large and enclosed in leathery cases. To shelter them from predators, or prevent them from drifting away, mother sharks deposit their eggs into crevices or attach them to seaweed or other structures by long, coiled filaments at their corners. You can sometimes find dogfish eggs on beaches at low tide. The rectangular, dark brown egg cases, about half the size of playing cards, are given the fanciful name "mermaid's purses."

Most sharks don't lay eggs but give birth to fully formed young, ready to survive on their own. There are different ways in which young sharks develop inside their mothers. In the most common sequence, the eggs hatch within the oviducts (tubes leading from the ovaries), and the embryos are at first nourished there by the remaining

egg yolk. As they grow, they feed on milklike fluids that the mother secretes from her oviduct walls.

The growing young of some species begin their predatory activities even before they are born. Among sand tigers, threshers, and makos, the largest hatchlings eat their smaller developing brothers and sisters, together with any remaining eggs, until there is only one survivor left in each oviduct.

A few shark species, including hammerheads, basking sharks, and requiem sharks, have pregnancies that are more like those of mammals than fish. The female shark produces a placentalike structure from her ovisac wall (an enlarged part of the oviduct) that connects her bloodstream with those of the embryos. The developing young are nourished directly from their

Swell sharks hatch from egg cases.

Mature female cat sharks tend to swim in deeper water.

mother's body through this structure until they are ready to be born.

Some live-young-bearing sharks can give birth to as many as sixty sharklets in a single litter, but most have much smaller numbers, some as few as one or two. Whether born live or hatched from eggs, the newly emerged sharks are on their own from the beginning, with no further help or protection from their mothers.

In many species, male and female sharks go their separate ways when they're not breeding. Young sharks, too, may live in different areas from their parents, where there is more food suitable to their size. Since big sharks eat smaller sharks, even of their own species, it is safer to swim with companions of a similar size. In the Caribbean Sea, for example, marbled cat sharks of different sexes and ages are generally found at different depths. Immature males favor shallow waters; immature females inhabit middle depths; and larger, mature females swim in deeper water. Adult males move into deep water only during the breeeding season. Other shark species, however, don't seem to segregate in any regular way.

Much is still unknown about the reproduction of most sharks, such as how long they take to develop from fertilized eggs to newborns, or at what age they first breed. In general, sharks grow slowly, mature late, and can live for many years. Gestation (the length of pregnancy) can be a year or longer, and some species may not breed every year. In many shark species, the females can store the males' sperm inside their bodies for several months after mating. This lets them control the time of fertilization, perhaps waiting until they are in peak condition.

Some shark species are known to live for a hundred years or longer and are not mature enough to breed until they are twenty years old. Male whale sharks are thought to take thirty years before reaching breeding condition. This means they must survive being caught or killed for a good part of their lives before they even have a chance to reproduce. It's a fact of shark life that now puts many sharks in danger of extinction at the hands of the most formidable predators of all – humans.

Saving Sharks

Feared and misunderstood, sharks have been quietly disappearing from the oceans with hardly a voice raised to protect them. Hunted without mercy, more than 100 million sharks are killed each year. The relentless slaughter has made some species extremely rare, and many others today face the same fate, including makos, threshers, lemon sharks, and hammerheads.

With their slow rates of growth and reproduction, sharks cannot easily recover from such intense pressure. Populations of sharks hard hit by commercial fisheries earlier this century have still not regained their numbers nearly fifty years after fishing boats stopped pursuing them.

Shark fishing goes back a long time. During the 1600s and 1700s, basking sharks were caught off the coast of Cape Cod to supply oil for the lamps of settlers. A single large shark liver yields more than 100 gallons of oil. Sharks have also been hunted in various parts of the world for their meat and as a source of medicines, vitamins, and cosmetics. In China, their fins are a traditional ingredient in shark fin soup. Sharks' teeth are used for weapons and jewelry, and shark skin is used as a substitute for sandpaper. Shark skin is also cured and made into such goods as purses, shoes, and wallets.

During World War II, shark oil came back in demand as petroleum prices rose and was especially valued as a lubricant for aircraft engines. More recently, sharks have been used to make fish meal and animal feed. Shark cartilage was popularized in the 1980s as a possible treatment for cancer and is now sold in many pharmacies.

In addition to the sharks killed by commercial fisheries, growing numbers of sharks are being caught by recreational fishers. Fishing for sharks with a hook and line has become more popular as traditional game

Relentless shark fishing has made lemon sharks like this one increasingly rare.

BIG AND SMALL

For the very biggest of animals, ocean life has a great advantage. The buoyant force of salt water helps support their great bulk, so an ocean-living giant needs a less massive skeleton to brace it, and less massive muscles to move it, than a similar-size animal on land. The largest sea creatures today outweigh any animal that has ever lived on land, although some of the biggest dinosaurs probably came close.

In general, big animals are more likely to be plant eaters. From the extinct Diplodocus to modern elephants, blue whales, and whale sharks, the largest bulks are fueled by browsing. One reason may be that plant food is more plentiful and takes less energy to obtain than animal food.

Size and fierceness do not always go hand in

hand. Although the great white shark is both large and fierce, the whale shark is even larger but extremely placid. One of the fiercest sharks is a twenty-inch monster called the cookie-cutter shark. Using razor-sharp teeth, it will attack and bite chunks of flesh from whales more than twenty times its length.

Comparing animals of different sizes, biologists have developed a set of mathematical relationships known as allometric laws. These describe how different characteristics of animals vary with their body size. From insects to whales, these rules of biological design predict certain features of an animal's life with amazing accuracy. For example, as bodies get bigger, hearts beat more slowly, energy is used more efficiently, and lifetimes are longer.

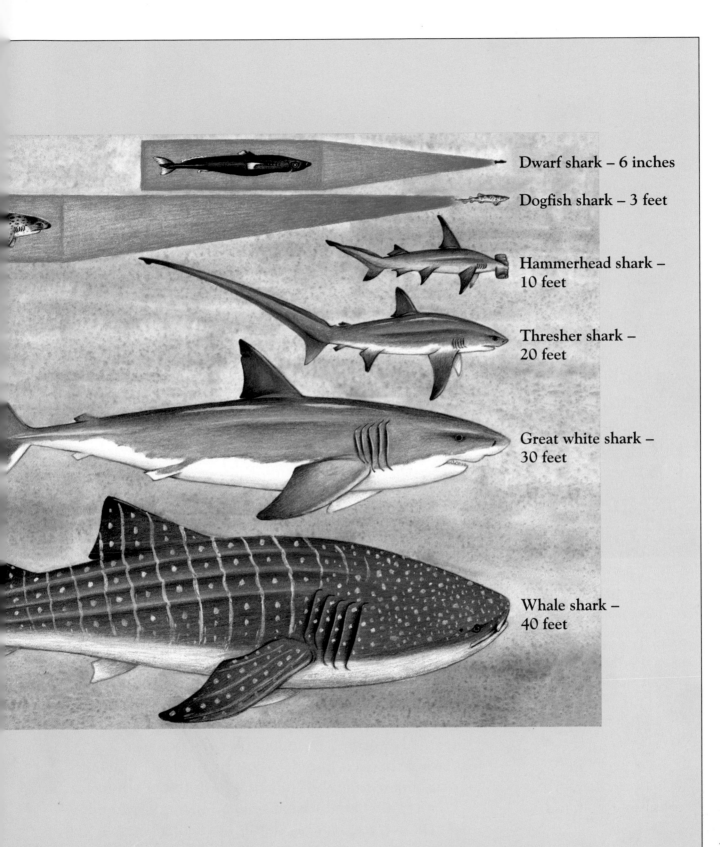

Dwarf shark – 6 inches

Dogfish shark – 3 feet

Hammerhead shark – 10 feet

Thresher shark – 20 feet

Great white shark – 30 feet

Whale shark – 40 feet

Millions of sharks, like this blue shark, become entangled in fishing nets each year.

fish, such as marlin, tuna, and swordfish, have become less plentiful.

Millions more sharks die each year after getting tangled in gill nets and drift nets set to catch other fish. Unable to breathe if they cannot move, netted sharks quickly die of suffocation. In most cases, these accidentally caught sharks are simply cut loose and discarded. Another wasteful and cruel practice taking its toll of sharks is finning – cutting the fins off living sharks and tossing the animals back into the sea to die.

Because of their large size and habit of swimming near the surface, basking sharks have long been viewed as a menace by the fishing industry. A single shark caught up in fishing gear can cause a lot of expensive damage. Also, many believe that basking sharks compete with salmon and cod for the same food. With too many basking sharks in an area, the industry argues, there will be fewer of these other valuable fish. Responding to salmon fishery complaints, the Canadian government for many years killed basking sharks off its west coast by ramming them with ships fitted with sharp steel bows.

To know how seriously a shark population is threatened, scientists need to know how many there are, how quickly they grow, and how many young they produce. It's very difficult to get this information about sharks. How can you observe and follow an animal that lives in the open ocean?

One technique scientists are using to study sharks is to label them, attaching a numbered plastic tag, about twelve inches long and as thick as a pencil, to the shark's back near its dorsal fin. Gentle, slow-moving species, such as whale sharks, are tagged in the water by divers. Others have to be caught first and then released. At the same time, the shark's size is recorded, with the date and place of tagging. When a tagged shark is later caught, or seen by other divers, scientists learn how far it has traveled and how much it has grown. Tagging also helps researchers determine how long sharks live.

If sharks are to survive, there must be limits on the numbers caught and killed each year. But hunting isn't the only threat to their future. Pollution of the oceans also endangers sharks and other marine creatures. Many of the chemicals that pollute the land and air eventually find their way into the oceans, washed there from streams and rivers and brought down in rainfall. The breeding areas of sharks, in shallow waters around coastlines, are especially at risk from this hazard. Pollutants may affect the fertility of adult sharks or damage the health and development of their growing young. Pollution can also reduce the numbers of smaller fish on which sharks feed.

43

Education is slowly changing public attitudes toward sharks. Once seen only as brutal eating machines, sharks are now thought of by more and more people as remarkable animals vital to marine ecosystems. Most educational of all, perhaps, are first-hand encounters, organized as part of the growing demand for ecotourist activities. In the warm waters off western Australia, for example, many people pay for the chance to dive near spectacular and harmless whale sharks. Another popular destination for shark viewing is the Bahamas, where 21,000 sport divers went on shark-watching dives during 1994.

We can't all get to see sharks for ourselves, however. And no aquariums have yet been successful in keeping or breeding large sharks in captivity. Captured open-sea sharks rarely survive for long. They usually refuse food and may simply lie on the bottom of their tank until they die. Even when kept in large, circular tanks where they can swim continuously, sharks tend to bang into the sides and injure themselves.

If we persist in slaughtering sharks faster than they can reproduce, species that have lived on Earth for millions of years may vanish within the lifetime of today's children. Why should we care? There are selfish reasons. Shark studies have recently helped medical researchers learn a lot about immune systems, offering hope of new techniques for treating cancer. Sharks also play an important role in the ocean's ecology. As top predators in many food chains, they help maintain healthy populations of other fish, keeping diverse and balanced populations of many other species in the largest ecosystems on the planet. Above all, perhaps, our world would become a much poorer and emptier place if there were no longer sharks swimming the oceans.

The massive and gentle whale shark attacts tourists eager to see these impressive animals.

INDEX